About *Permanent Change of Station*

"Lisa Stice's new poetry collection, *Permanent Change of Station,* is spare and lovely. Shadowed by deployments and military moves, Stice demonstrates how the smallest, most tenuous moments in life can illustrate a family's larger joys and fears."

—Siobhan Fallon, author of
You Know When the Men Are Gone
and *The Confusion of Languages*

"By using a language stripped down to its basics, one that plays philosophically with the meanings of military terminologies, Lisa Stice produces a cartography of domestic space that is riddled with loss. As seen throughout her new collection, the war for Blue Star families is a war between remembrance and loneliness. Stice celebrates the moms and kids who 'hold down the fort' back home, expressing awe at all the ways they find to survive and thrive."

—Lynn Marie Houston, author of the poetry collections
Unguarded and *The Mauled Keeper*

"The experiences [Lisa Stice] writes of—the losses and realizations—are part of a military life that often feels simultaneously impenetrable and inescapable. Absence, isolation, and relocation become habit we don't often read about, because part of us breaks in every move we do not choose, every uncertainty we are told to sustain; our "legs once strongpoints // now leave nothing left / to stand on". Stice's poems are knitted together by a tenderness that wants us to know it remembers every expectation, uprooting, and 'chime / of a simple life.'"

—Abby E. Murray, author of the poetry collections
How to Be Married After Iraq
and *Quick Draw: Poems from a Soldier's Wife*

"By often including borrowed text, Stice creates cento-like poems that seamlessly weave together found text with her own beautifully rendered images. One of my favorites is the poem, 'On Such Little Things Happiness Depends.' Here the words of Oscar Wilde and Sun Tzu slip into the space of bedtime lullaby as Stice and her daughter listen 'while the moth spreads / her brown wings and flies like a shadow / silent through the trees.'"

—Pamela Hart, author of the poetry collection
Mothers Over Nangarhar

"Lisa Stice's poems occupy a territory of the military family often missed in the public narrative of war. In these poems, she assumes the role of translator in connecting opposites: military and civilian, peace beneath the stars and the Blue Star of the deployed warrior's family, often suppressing anxiety to project calm for those who depend on it. These poems show the family, 'unsure of how to answer' questions of place—pulling identity from a pile of images and sounds—black-crowned herons, magnolias and moths, or, most importantly, the head on a shoulder and the dog lying at one's feet. These are images that serve to pull pieces together in a world sorely in need of connection."

—Dwight A. Gray, author of the poetry collections
Contested Terrain and *Overwatch*

"Lisa Stice makes magic in *Permanent Change of Station*. She can take a quiet moment and use it to express great tumult and upheaval; she can spy the signposts in life that point toward greater things, markers that the rest of us might miss. While reading this collection, I found the poems visiting me all throughout the day, found myself nodding, *yes*. Stice's work never disappoints. She has an eye for the little detail that will break your heart."

—Andria Williams, author of
The Longest Night: A Novel

"Read about the joyful love of a mother for her daughter and dog—but there's a price. You'll also experience what it's like to be related to Uncle Sam by marriage: gut-wrenching worry, isolation, and disruption. Stice channels Sun Tzu's *Art of War* into the title of one of her poems and reminds us: We Can Only Be Saved by Destruction."

—Eric Chandler, author of the poetry collection
Hugging This Rock: Poems of Earth & Sky, Love & War

"Lisa Stice's poetry resonates in the oft-unsounded silences of military life. It sings with the learned, quiet endurance of Marine Corps families who pack and unpack, tend the roots during every transplant, wait, tire of waiting, hope, know better than to hope, nurture their selfhood, and grow—because nature demands it. Her verse conjures presence in its very absence."

—William Schuth, poetry editor of the literary journal
The Deadly Writers Patrol

Permanent
Change of Station

Lisa Stice

Middle West Press LLC
Johnston, Iowa

Permanent Change of Station
Copyright © 2018 by Lisa Stice

Poetry / Subjects & Themes / Family & War

Stice, Lisa
     Permanent Change of Station / Lisa Stice
     ISBN (print): 978-0-9969317-6-2
     ISBN (e-book): 978-0-9969317-7-9
     Library of Congress Control Number: 2018938212

Middle West Press LLC
P.O. Box 31099
Johnston, Iowa 50131-9428
www.middlewestpress.com

Special thanks to James Burns of Aurora, Colo.
Your patronage helps publish great military-themed writing!
www.aimingcircle.com

Cover images:
"Little Girl in Blue Armchair" (1878)
by Mary Stevenson Cassatt (1844-1926)

U.S. Marine Corps photo (2017) by Sgt. Conner Robbins,
Task Force 51/5th Marine Expeditionary Brigade

Author photo by Andria Williams, *The Military Spouse Book Review*

For Saoirse & Seamus

CONTENTS

Half-Known Roads

PCS

Why do they say *permanent*?
It doesn't hold steady,
but then neither do mountains
nor bridges nor brick houses
nor anything else.

They say, *Go. Adapt.*
Now we understand—
we're permanently changed.
That can be counted on,
and we change often.

Orders Received

Once there was a girl,
and she lived in a house.

She knew that house
and loved that house.

She would crawl up its stairs,
sleep in its rooms,

imagine its walls a forest
and gather the leaves.

But time went by.

She would be taken
far away from here.

She gathered her things:
stuffed tea party guests,

glue and paint,
chariots and armor.

The house knew the girl
would not come back again.

Support

This great honor
comes with mixed feelings:

sacrifices,
efforts,

time,
the force that we have

to operate independently:
capable,

peaceful,
this invasion

into the personal.
Long-term success depends on

significant milestones,
the efforts of all.

Recognize the efforts—
support them,

meet expectations.

Where Are You From?

In my pause, I must seem strange
or stupid. But I am unsure
of how to answer—where I was born,
where I lived the longest, from where
I most recently traveled,
where I felt most at home?
When you are no longer a toddler,
you will be asked the same,
a typical first day of school survey.
You will pause, too,
unsure of how to answer.

Answer: Just Empty

Question: What do you call
the dents where
tables, sofas, beds
used to be?

Is It for This

men board armored cruisers, C-130s
earn salaries, ranks
for the protection of—

chalk hearts, hopscotch squares
washed away in rain
sidewalks stained in pastel

boxes of melted crayons
melted a little more
inside a moving truck

birthday streamers
still rolled up somewhere
in a box under a box behind a box

locking a door
another last time
with no good-byes

a girl in a hotel crib
not her blanket
her dog on guard

interstates like gray snapshots
where we lose our way

Defrosting

I will return to the desert,
prickly heat warming my blood.

When the snowflakes failed to melt
on my shoulders, I knew it was time.

I had already lost my scarf,
lost friends who stopped calling

after a few months, lost
my great-grandfather's prayer book

somewhere amongst
do-it-yourself manuals, lost sleep,

lost money, lost my taste
for spicy foods and cold beer,

nearly lost my voice, and nearly
lost my footing that night

I slid down the sloped sidewalk,
leaving you frozen in that moment.

Distance and Security

we are at play
we are in a house
on a pretend road

either to safety
or ruin—around
and around

and around
the kitchen island
going away

going away fast
we believe
we are far away

earth is made
of distances
great and small

when we are far
away, we believe
we are near

Walking Backwards

you walk in reverse
all around the furniture
the game of the day

I'd like to pretend
these backwards steps
could order this rain

back to the ocean
pull the pale sun
from its hiding place

behind gray clouds
we could all retreat
a backwards march

until we're on our
hands and knees
crawling back

to fuzzy sight
and muffled sounds
the moment we were received

Homes Will Be Stripped Bare

this is one world
and this is another
the borders merely

traced out on the ground
with a small stick
in one world, animals:

zebras, giraffes,
lions, horses,
and dinosaurs

bide their time
stand together
quietly encamped

kept in readiness
for a decision
made in a single day

to overthrow their kingdom
cause commotion at home
the animals know

there is no time to ponder
just march to the place
beyond ordinary rules

The Dog Speaks

He says, *I can't leave.*
This place is mine—
I claimed all the trees.

I say, *There will be more.*
After all the temporary homes
and all the stops in between,

this whole country
will be yours.

Fifth Choice

I'd be
lying

if I
told you

*we get
what we
deserve*

When in Difficult Country

join hands
where roads intersect

I am versed in the art
of varying plans

look both ways
do not linger

we do not know
the mountains

and valleys ahead
we never will

they are earth and stones
just the same

Our Nine Situations

1. *dispersive ground*
   the sea shells we found here
   look like the ones from there

2. *facile ground*
   all unpacked boxes remain
   stacked in the garage

3. *contentious ground*
   where we want to be forever
   waits until retirement

4. *open ground*
   we can say where we'd like to go
   and just hope it's assigned

5. *ground of intersecting highways*
   there is school, vacations, dance
   there is training, last-minute departures

6. *serious ground*
   relatives are voices on the phone
   people we see twice a year

7. *difficult ground*
   no, Daddy won't be there
   yes, we thought he would be

8. *hemmed-in ground*
    you keep me occupied
    tiara crafts, invisible baked goods

9. *desperate ground*
    we call this our home
    even though it isn't

Resolve

raise two regiments
equal care

appoint
enlist

such good
or so acquainted

to serve
advantage by sea

require
enlist

commission
to serve for war
      dismiss

Come Along

sunny spots can be abandoned
but I know it's hard to stir forth
an insubordination of natural
tendencies   a disorganization
like the rustling of wings
as the bird hurls itself against
a storm   flies a great distance
over the hills to somewhere   to
accessible ground   reoccupy

Lisa Stice

The Box Maze Swallows a Birthday

From the big truck
men carry boxes
build boxwalls

narrow paths
we will walk for months.

Our dog lies in the yard
chin resting heavy on paws
he watches

the maze grow box by box.
The air is thick with summer
fire ants walk in lines.

You, in too-big dress
and too-big sandals,
sit next to your dog-brother

raise a cup of water
to a mouth that hasn't spoken
since we arrived here.

This is your second birthday
but there is only more boxes
ant bites swell to the size of quarters.

Reduction

at the bottom of the box
we found the broken pieces
separate parts of a whole

the importance of a ceramic
elephant reduced to sharp
edges   dust   disconnected

system of reliability of
expectation and memory
legs once strongpoints

now leave nothing left
to stand on   a memory
to throw away and forget

Lisa Stice

All This and More Will Be Discovered Together

How does this all work into our lives,
into the plans we made? Who are we?

The In-Betweens

Another Disappointment

You imagined
foxgloves
quite differently.

Backyard Play

this was different
from where they came
so they built defenses

walled cities
of empty shoe boxes
the piling up of pine cones

they went into a corner
talked about it together—
this strange place

as she petted his back
as he turned to lick her cheek
they forgot to be frightened

Father's Day

It's just
the three of us

      mother
      daughter
      dog

again.

Lisa Stice

View from My Kitchen Window

a cardinal, showy red
on the branch of a bare tree
sits like an idol—

how I envy the plumage,
the hollowness of bones
the easy lift from its perch

Winter Torpor

Gray sunlight intrudes
my room, so I pull the covers
tighter. Bits of last night's dinner
crusts on plates and forks, dust
slumbers on furniture
and Depression glass,
the yellowing weeping fig
loses another leaf,
but none are enough to lift
my face from its dent in the pillow.
I know my husband has already
eaten egg whites and yogurt, run three miles
and left for work two hours
ago. My terrier's whining
bedside petitions open my eyes
enough to see the supplicating
Joshua tree outside my window.
Its spiny arms point desperately in all directions,
but I shut my eyes.

Lisa Stice

Learning to Speak

in the morning—
night night gone
Dada shoe gone
Dada gone

at meal time—
Dada gone
food gone
milk gone

on the weekend—
bird gone
car gone
Dada gone

in remembrance—
dance gone
sun gone
all gone

Somehow We Knew

holding out advantages
until confirmation
word sent from great

distances that you would
change each day

grow taller and need
me less—fall asleep
with just a kiss

the order arrived
and you followed it

instinct to keep you
small to keep you mine
but even the sharpest

weapons grow dull
remain behind untaken

Remember

we pressed the dough flat
readied it for cutting

our hands shiny
with butter and shortening

it was Christmas
or maybe it was Easter

Such Is the Art of Warfare

Sometimes her mother would worry
about her, that she would be lonesome
all by herself, with a dog for a brother

in this out of the way place
where we are only acquainted
with neighbors, and only some.

This is the art of studying circumstances.

She pitched up camp
between sofa and coffee table
under pillows and cushions

she said, *I like it better here.*
She liked to smell the flowers
hand-picked from air

hold their invisible petals
against her face, breathe
the scent of once upon a time.

This is the art of studying moods.

And so her mother knew
she was not lonesome:
she was like a mountain

like a fire, like a thunderbolt.
Her mother whispered,
let your plans be impenetrable.

This is the art of self-preservation.

Because Everything Else Is Quite Unequal

The goats push begging noses
through chain link
                        you ration
out alfalfa pellets
                        let them
receive their fair shares
from your upturned palms.

Looking Up

One contrail scars the cloudless sky.
Four months have brought no rain.
The sparrows and the locusts fly.
One contrail scars the cloudless sky.
Four months have brought no rain.

Calling Attention

The spoken word
does not carry far enough: hence

> kazoo parades
> harmonica parades
> recorder parades

> tap shoes

> anything can be drummed
> a fist becomes a microphone

> feigned sneezes
> feigned coughs

> *hear me, right now*

Ordinary objects
cannot be seen well enough: hence

> a bed conquered
> by stuffed animals

> *one, two, three, four,*
> *five, six, eighteen, nineteen,*
> *here I come*

Lisa Stice

a tower ten blocks tall
a paper colored red

the dog draped
in ribbons

watch me, right now

Fix, Mommy

Some things just never
go back to the way they were.

Afternoon One Day When You Were Young

It is nearly autumn's end, but
we wear short-sleeve t-shirts
and light denim, and you
with the feather-lite hair
the color of maple syrup
and pancakes, you chase
your Norwich Terrier brother
who chases squirrels
through loblolly pines,
his barks louder and shriller
than the call of a tea kettle,
and this is the day I want
to pause, to fold up like a card,
open when you are taller
and no longer spin past dizziness.

In the Evening

My heart beats
to the tune
of glasses—
washed clean,
free of spots,
a clear reflection of myself—
clinking in the sink,
the humble song
of glorias,
the chime
of a simple life.

Daughter

we are raising fire
a shock-headed girl
in this cold season

when you start a fire
be to windward, wait
for it to break out within

mind now what I say
remain quiet
for when fire breaks

we call these special days
nothing to me is sweeter
than a crackling flame

Growth Chart

every time
I see you
        you're taller

Lisa Stice

The Need of War

you are too little
I am too big

I lift you to the switch
turn on the light
and you are happy

this is what you will wear
this is what you will eat
it is now time to take a bath

you stick a black olive
on the end of each finger
and want me to join
but I just can't do that

here is your chair
like none of the others
it's hard for you to accept this

the things I took for granted
the things you took for granted
laid out in the open now

you are too young
I am too old

There Is a Proper Season

when flowers are fresh in the field
when daddies are ordinary men
when we fall behind in chores
and just sit and drink lemonade

Credit for Courage

Bugs scare me.

Did you know
lizards eat bugs?

Lizards love me.

New Trick

Wave bye-bye.
The dog raises a shaky paw
receives a treat.

Bedtime Stories

Blue Girl

April is the month of the military child
of gray clouds and drizzle, days spent indoors

daily struggles and sacrifices unnoticed
drawn out in crayon on white paper

girl with a blue scribble where a face should be
floats above a house without a roof

sing out in rhyme—
where's the white bunny?

where's the gray fox?
wrapped up in brown tissue

asleep in a box
steadfast child whom I depend upon

whose smile I coax to help me cope
put away the crayons, it's time for a nap

Half-known War

flowers fall
poor things

dying one by one
dried now

I dream his face is stars
nocturnal flowers

unsubdued and burned
like warm wounds

stars fade   nothing

What Are You Scared Of?

I was walking in the night
And I saw nothing scary.
For I have never been afraid
Of anything. Not very.
                    —Dr. Seuss, *What Was I Scared Of?*

The glow of the night light,
shadows taller than walls
so tall they bend and look down
from the ceiling.

Shadows pool and change
even the most familiar faces—
Dog Dog, Rainbow Brite,
Lambie, Thumper.

Light off!

Darkness is just
sleep before dreams,
peek-a-boo before the boo,
what we see when we hug.

On Such Little Things Happiness Depends

You say, *Stop singing*, lean your head
on my shoulder, begin your own lullaby—

secret system of your voice like bubbling water,
divine manipulation of threads

woven through wind and kissed by stars,
secret pieces of news divulged to the night.

The black-crowned heron builds
his nest out of music by moonlight.

Coyotes march from great distances,
the door-keepers and sentries of the dark.

Magnolia blossoms as big as the cold
crystal moon lean down their sweet scent

and listen while the moth spreads
her brown wings and flies like a shadow

silent through the trees. Night after night
you sing your story to the stars

until you drop down exhausted on your bed
and your little dog lies down at your feet.

The Book Closes

words become a strange
dream   an explosion
the releasing of the trigger
another shovelful of earth
to plant secrets   a storm
breaking with the momentum
of a round stone and yet
no real disorder at all
just the melodies that can never
be heard   the colors
that can never be seen
just like the little birds
that fly far away   further
than we will ever know

Advantages

When we are children,
we learn to be invisible—

disappear behind hands,
under blankets,
behind doors.

Where did you go?
Divine art of secrecy—

Water shapes its course
to the nature of the ground

and we learn how to act
from mimicking words
watching quietly

from high up
on Daddy's shoulders.

Conquer

you spin the globe
slow it to a sliding stop
controlling the world with a finger

Blue Star Family

Those stars weren't so big. They were really so small.
You might think such a thing wouldn't matter at all.
—Dr. Seuss, The Sneetches

Our backs pressed against
Bermuda grass in our backyard

we blew out those stars
one by one, just as easy as

candle flames or dandelion fuzz
until the sky was dark enough
to let us *sleep tight.*

Watchdog

while Daddy patrols
someone else's night

here, you assume the role
of our point-man—

      the first to enter rooms
      ears alert and turning
      listening for the unfamiliar

      a sentry to sit before us
      to bark a signal
      detain our fears

Secure

ease into my arms
that fear is only
the noise of thunder

strongly garrisoned
by lullabies and stories
we build our defensive

A Thing to Carry

[...] when the army is restless and distrustful, trouble is sure to come [...]
—Sun Tzu, "Attacks by Stratagem," *The Art of War*

take this with you
this kiss

after you walk
the long passageway

after you lose
clear sight of childhood

after you learn
life is quite unequal

warmth left by a kiss
will be a relic

Like Pennies

if only we could
plunk minutes, seconds

into mason jars
let them collect

on a shelf beside
ebony elephants

framed photos
aging books

if only we could
open those jars

when we need the time
but we can't

The Dog Dreams

After a while, when nothing happened,
they began to get restless.
> —Michael Bond, *Paddington*

In consequence of heavy rains,
you must wait until it subsides—
lay down your body, small
and furry, close your eyes.

> You pass quickly over mountains,
> keep company in the neighborhood of valleys.
> Wind your way through tangled thickets,
> hollow basins filled with reeds,
> woods thick with undergrowth.
> With each bound, birds rise
> in their flight, startled beasts retreat.

I run my hand along your side—
Where are you going in such a hurry?
Come home and stay.
The sun is shining.

Lisa Stice

So Much for Knowing What to Say

What this?
Why tree far away?
Where Daddy?
Why need go?
When food?

the signs—
I should have
expected this invasion

and then my weak
defense—

a letter
it grows old and tall
at work
we have to
when it's ready

After a Nightmare

we inventory stuffed sentries
check windows and doors

when all is secure and sound
hug, kiss, say *good night* again

Lisa Stice

We Can Only Be Saved by Destruction

there was a little harbor
a place to be quiet
at low tide you stepped

into the water up to
your waist and just
tried to look beyond
the horizon to glimpse

the world you belonged to
human nature wants
a refuge but

you will leave
there is no help for it

When Your Substance Is Drained Away

hold out   sometimes
victory is long in coming
there is nothing we can do
to stop the sunny places
from turning cold   put
on your mittens wear
a sweater tuck in the blanket
edges   the seasons
make way for each other

Home Gets Confusing

Lion and Tiger forgot where each lived
and found themselves together.

Bookcase

This is where we keep history
on these shelves just so high—
you make your own selections.

Story-books and lesson-books
mixed together and seen as same,
we open them and read the words

build a language that speaks
volumes. *Why?* answered
by kittens, billy goats and

girls who make their homes
in hollow trees, familiar
children lost in the woods.

Lisa Stice

And Then We Didn't Think about That Anymore

sometimes what lies in our hands
leaves us goes off somewhere
hides in the most secret places

I should have told you
I could have explained this
how the things we know go away

ACKNOWLEDGEMENTS

I am grateful to the editors of the following literary magazines, in which some of these poems first appeared—some in slightly different versions:

"**Afternoon One Day When You Were Young**" first appeared in *The Magnolia Review*, Vol. 2, No. 2, Winter 2016

"**Backyard Play**" first appeared in *Poetry Super Highway's* "Poet of the Week" feature Oct. 3-9, 2016

"**Because Everything Else Is Quite Unequal**" first appeared in *Poetry Super Highway's* "Poet of the Week" feature Oct. 3-9, 2016

"**Blue Girl**" first appeared in *Sheila-Na-Gig*, Vol. 1, No. 3, Spring 2017

"**The Book Closes**" first appeared in *The Wrath-Bearing Tree*, January 2018

"**The Box Maze Swallows a Birthday**" first appeared in *Shantih Journal*, Vol. 2, No. 1, Spring 2017

"**Daughter**" first appeared in *The Wrath-Bearing Tree*, January 2018

"**Defrosting**" first appeared in *Split Rock Review*, No. 6, Spring 2016

"**Distance and Security**" first appeared in *Collateral*, No. 1, Autumn 2016

"**The Dog Dreams**" first appeared in *Shantih Journal*, Vol. 2, No. 1, Spring 2017

"**Half-known War**" first appeared in *The Deadly Writers Patrol*, No. 11, Autumn 2016

"**Homes Will Be Stripped Bare**" first appeared in *The Wrath-Bearing Tree*, January 2018

"**Is It for This**" first appeared in *Random Sample Review*, February 2016

"**Learning to Speak**" first appeared in *GFT Presents: One in Four*, Vol. 1, No. 2 , November 2016

"The Need of War" first appeared in *The Irish Literary Review*, Autumn 2016

"On Such Little Things Happiness Depends" first appeared in *Inklette*, No. 3, Summer 2016

"Our Nine Situations" first appeared in *Skylight 47*, No. 7, September 2016

"PCS" first appeared in *Collateral*, No. 1, Autumn 2016

"Reduction" first appeared in *The Magnolia Review*, Vol. 2, No. 2, Winter 2016

"Such Is the Art of Warfare" first appeared in *Shantih Journal*, Vol. 2, No. 1, Spring 2017

"Support" first appeared in *The Deadly Writers Patrol*, No. 11, Autumn 2016

"View from My Kitchen Window" first appeared in *Fredericksburg Literary and Art Review*, Vol. 4, No. 1, Spring 2016

"Walking Backwards" first appeared in *Peeking Cat Poetry Magazine*, No. 20, December 2016

"When in Difficult Country" first appeared in *Into the Void Magazine*, No. 1, July 2016

"When Your Substance Is Drained Away" first appeared in *The Magnolia Review*, Vol. 2, No. 2, Winter 2016

"Winter Torpor" first appeared in *Peeking Cat Poetry Magazine*, No. 16, August 2016

NOTES

In my first poetry collection, *Uniform* (Aldrich Press, 2016), I experiment with the poetry of erasure—cutting poems out of military briefings, speeches, and literature I encountered while navigating my found realities as a woman married to a United States Marine. Erasure of these texts provided me with a sense of control at times when I most felt my life controlled by the Corps, and it helped me to carve my place within tradition.

Close readers of *Permanent Change of Station* may detect a different technique, that of borrowed language and phrases. While I continue to speak and translate the strange dialect that permeates military life, my gaze has expanded to include texts found in my home library. In a new environment far from friends and family, I build a community of words by weaving my own with those of Sun Tzu and classic children's book writers. It is a community located somewhere between civilian and military, a place where military dependents reside.

All chapter titles or excerpts from *The Art of War* by Sun Tsu are language taken from the 1910 translation by Lionel Giles.

To ensure full disclosure and translation, in addition to explaining some of the military jargon, I give credit here to the words that have inspired my own:

Half-Known Roads

The name of this section is taken from the last two words of World War I poet Wilfred Owen's 1918 poem "The Send-Off."

"PCS": "Permanent Change of Station" is the military phrase used to describe receiving orders to move one's household and duty location.

"Orders Received": Some words in this poem are borrowed from *The Giving Tree* by Shel Silverstein ("Once there was a tree"; "would gather her leaves"; "and the boy loved the house"; "But time went by"; "take me far away from here") and from the chapter "Waging War" in *The Art of War* by Sun Tzu ("the expenditure at home and at the front, including entertainment of guests, small items such as glue and paint, and sums spent on chariots and armor"; "victory is long in coming").

"Distance and Security": Some words in this poem are borrowed from *Go, Dog. Go!* by P.D. Eastman ("at play"; "a house"; "around and around and around"; "going away"; "going away fast") and from the chapter "Laying Plans" in *The Art of War* by Sun Tzu ("a road either to safety or to ruin"; "great and small"; "danger and security"; "when we are near, we must make the enemy believe we are far away; when far away, we must make him believe we are near").

"Homes Will Be Stripped Bare": Some words in this poem are borrowed from the chapters "Weak Points and Strong" ("the lines of our encampment be merely traced out on the ground"; "quietly encamped"); "The Attack by Fire" ("bide your time"; "kept in readiness"); "The Use of Spies" ("there will be commotion at home"); "Attacks by Stratagem" ("overthrows their kingdom"); "Maneuvering" ("ponder before you make a move"); "Laying Plans" ("beyond the ordinary rules"); and "Waging War" (the homes of the people will be stripped bare") in *The Art of War* by Sun Tzu.

"When in Difficult Country": Some words in this poem are borrowed from the story "Two Large Stones," found in the picture book *Mouse Soup* by Arnold Lobel ("we do not know"; "we never will"; "mountains and valleys"; "earth and stones"; "looks just the same") and from the chapter "Variation of Tactics" in *The Art of War* by Sun Tzu ("When in difficult country"; "where high roads intersect"; "join hands"; "do not linger"; "unversed in the art if varying his plans").

"Our Nine Situations": The title and some words of this poem are borrowed from the chapter "The Nine Situations" in *The Art of War* by Sun Tzu ("The Nine Situations"; "1. dispersive ground"; "2. facile ground"; "3. contentious ground"; "4. open ground"; "5. ground of intersecting highways"; "6. serious ground"; "7. difficult ground" "8. hemmed-in ground"; "9. desperate ground").

"Come Along": Some words in this poem are borrowed from the story "The Vagabonds" by The Brothers Grimm ("come along"; "over the hills"; "rustling of wings") and from the chapter "Terrain" in *The Art of War* by Sun Tzu ("accessible ground"; "a great distance"; "sunny spots"; "can be abandoned but hard to reoccupy"; "to stir forth"; "insubordination"; "disorganization"; "hurled against").

"Reduction": Some words in this poem are borrowed from the chapter "Weak Points and Strong" in *The Art of War* by Sun Tzu ("separate parts of a whole")

The In-Betweens

"Backyard Play": Some words in this poem are borrowed from "Chapter VII in which Kanga and Baby Roo Come to the Forest, and Piglet Has a Bath" in *Winnie-the-Pooh* by A. A. Milne ("Nobody seemed to know where they came from, but they were in the Forest"; "went into a corner"; "forgot to be frightened") and from the chapter "Attacks by Stratagem" The Art of War by Sun Tzu ("walled cities," "the piling up of mounds").

"Somehow We Knew": Some words in this poem are borrowed from the chapters "Weak Points and Strong" ("holding out advantages"; "may march great distances"); "The Attack by Fire" ("follow it"); "Waging War" ("weapons will grow dull"), and "Attacks by Stratagem" ("remains untaken") in *The Art of War* by Sun Tzu.

"Such Is the Art of Warfare": Some words in this poem are borrowed from *The Story of Ferdinand* by Munro Leaf ("Once upon a time";

"liked to sit quietly and smell the flowers"; "he would sit in the shade all day and smell the flowers"; "Sometimes his mother [...] would worry about him"; "She was afraid he would be lonesome all by himself"; "'I like it better here'") and from the chapter "Maneuvering" in *The Art of War* by Sun Tzu ("pitching his camp"; "out of the way"; "we are acquainted"; "our neighbors"; "be like a fire"; "like a mountain"; "let your plans be dark and impenetrable as night"; "fall like a thunderbolt").

"Because Everything Else Is Quite Unequal": Part of this poem's title ("quite unequal") is borrowed from the chapter "Attacks by Stratagem" in *The Art of War* by Sun Tzu.

"Calling Attention": Some words in this poem are borrowed from the chapter "Maneuvering" in *The Art of War* by Sun Tzu ("The spoken word does not carry far enough: hence"; "Ordinary objects cannot be seen well enough: hence").

"Daughter": Some words in this poem are borrowed from the 1845 children's moral-driven nursery book *Struwwelpeter* translated by Heinrich Hoffman ("any thing to me is sweeter"; "shock-headed peter"; "they crackle so, and spit, and flame"; "mind now, Conrad, what I say") and the chapter "The Attack by Fire" in *The Art of War* by Sun Tzu ("material for raising fire"; "special days"; "days of rising wind"; "when fire breaks"; "remain quiet"; "wait for it to break out within"; "when you start a fire, be to windward").

"There Is a Proper Season": Some words in this poem are borrowed from the chapters "Weak Points and Strong" ("fresh in the field"); "The Attack by Fire" ("there is a proper season"); "The Use of Spies" ("ordinary men"); and "Maneuvering" ("fall behind") in *The Art of War* by Sun Tzu.

"Credit for Courage": The title is a phrase borrowed from the chapter "Tactical Dispositions" in *The Art of War* by Sun Tzu.

Bedtime Stories

"On Such Little Things Happiness Depends": Some words in this poem are borrowed from the 1888 children's short story "The Nightingale and the Rose" found in *The Happy Prince and Other Tales* by Oscar Wilde ("nest"; "on what little things does happiness depend"; "secrets of philosophy are mine"; "night after night I have told his story to the stars"; "silent, "spread her brown wings"; "passed through the grove like a shadow"; "built out of music by moonlight"; "voice like water bubbling"; "and the cold crystal moon leaned down and listened") and from the chapter "The Use of Spies" in *The Art of War* by Sun Tzu. ("marching them great distances"; "drop down exhausted in the highways"; "secret system"; "divine manipulation of the threads"; "cannot make certain of the truth"; "secret piece of news divulged"; "door-keepers and sentries").

"The Book Closes": Some words in this poem are borrowed from the 1835 short story "The Traveling Companion" by Hans Christian Andersen, translated by Erik Christian Haugaard ("he dreamed a strange dream"; "another shovelful of earth"; "the words became a picture"; "the little birds flew far into the world"; "the storm broke") and from the chapter "Energy" in *The Art of War* by Sun Tzu ("give rise to more melodies than can ever be heard"; "more hues than can ever be seen"; "releasing of the trigger"; "and yet no real disorder at all"; "the momentum of a round stone").

"Advantages": Some words in this poem are borrowed from the picture book *Good Night, Little Bear* by Patricia Scarry ("Bear swings his little one high up to his shoulders"; "sits high up in his father's shoulders and grins") and from the chapter "Weak Points and Strong" in *The Art of*

War by Sun Tzu ("O divine art of subtlety and secrecy"; "we learn to be invisible"; "Water shapes its course according to the nature of the ground").

Blue Star Family: A reference to a "Blue Star" has come to mean having a family member who is currently enlisted in the U.S. Armed Forces. The term has its origins in small, red-bordered "service flags" displayed on family homes. First used in World War I, these feature one star for each family member enlisted in service. "Gold Stars" indicate family members who have been killed while in uniformed service. While lesser known, "Silver Stars" indicate family members who have been injured and disabled while in uniformed service.

"Secure": Some words in this poem are borrowed from the chapter "Tactical Dispositions" ("secure"; "the noise of thunder") and "Terrain" ("strongly garrisoned") in *The Art of War* by Sun Tzu.

"A Thing to Carry": In addition to the epigraph, some words in this poem are borrowed from the chapter "Attacks by Stratagem" in *The Art of War* by Sun Tzu ("quite unequal").

"The Dog Dreams": In addition to the epigraph, some words in this poem are borrowed from *Paddington* by Michael Bond ("small and furry"; "come home and stay"; "The sun was shining") and from the chapter "The Army on the March" in *The Art of War* by Sun Tzu ("Pass quickly over mountains, and keep in the neighborhood of valleys"; "in consequence of heavy rains [...] you must wait until it subsides"; "tangled thickets"; "hollow basins filled with reeds"; "woods with thick undergrowth"; "rising birds in their flight"; "startled beasts").

"We Can Only Be Saved by Destruction": Some words in this poem are borrowed from the 1930 book *The Tale of Little Pig Robinson* by Beatrix Potter ("there was a little harbor"; "at low tide"; "she belonged to"; "you will leave") and from the chapter "The Nine Situations" in *The Art of War* by Sun Tzu ("we can only be saved by destruction"; "refuge"; "there is no help for it"; "to be quiet"; "human nature").

"When Your Substance Is Drained Away": Some words in this poem are borrowed from the chapters "Waging War" ("victory is long in coming"; "when their substance is drained away"); "The Army on the March" ("sunny places"); and "Weak Points and Strong" ("The four seasons make way for each other in turn") in *The Art of War* by Sun Tzu.

"And Then We Didn't Think about That Anymore": Some words in this poem are borrowed from the poem "Just Before We Begin", found in *When We Were Very Young* by A. A. Milne ("I should have told you"; "and then I didn't think about that anymore"; "I could have explained this") and from the chapter "Tactical Dispositions" in *The Art of War* by Sun Tzu ("lies in our own hands," "hides in the most secret recesses").

THANKS

Thanks to Randy Brown (*Welcome to FOB Haiku: War Poems from Inside the Wire*) for being enthusiastic about work in poetry long before this collection came about, and for hosting helpful "war writing" information at Red Bull Rising (**www.redbullrising.com**) and The Aiming Circle (**www.aimingcircle.com**). Even before we first met at the 2017 national conference Association of Writers & Writing Programs (AWP) in Washington, D.C. I already felt like I knew him. I'm grateful to have such a caring editor and colleague.

Thanks to my little muses, Saoirse and Seamus, for their endless inspiration.

Thanks to my husband for his editing eye and for his unconditional support.

Thanks to my parents, Lois and Robert Houlihan, and my brother, Patrick Houlihan, for being three of my loudest cheerleaders and for their encouragement. All of those bedtime stories that initiated my love of books are now being read to my book-loving kiddo. Thanks for being there since my very beginning.

Thanks to my Mesa State College (now Colorado Mesa University) creative writing professors who first introduced me to this poetic path: Diana Joseph (*I'm Sorry You Feel That Way*) and Randy Phillis (*Plots We Can't Keep Up With*).

Thanks to my University of Alaska Anchorage professors and mentors, who continue to teach me even after graduation: David Stevenson (*Warnings against Myself: Meditations on a Life in Climbing*); Linda McCarriston (*Eva-Mary*); Anne Caston (*Prodigal*); Zack Rogow (*Shipwrecked on a Traffic Island: And Other Previously Untranslated Gems*); and Elizabeth Bradfield (*Once Removed*).

Thanks to my fellow poets, fiction writers, and non-fiction writers who, through the low-residency Master of Fine Arts program at the University of Alaska, Anchorage, became fast friends and who continue to be a wonderful support network.

Thanks to my online writers group who provide valuable feedback and encouragement: Alice Jennings (*Katherine of Aragon*); Tara Ballard (*House of the Night Watch*); Chaun Ballard (*Flight*); Wendy Mannis Scher; Bobbie Scheide; Raquel Vasquez Gilliland (*Dirt and Honey*); Brieanna Lewis; Nicholas Vincent Miele; and Brandon Thompson.

Thanks to Vivian Wagner (*The Village*) and Kersten Christianson (*Something Yet to Be Named*) for heading The Daily Poet Writing Group.

Thanks to Andria Williams for founding and hosting *The Military Spouse Book Review* (**militaryspousebookreview.com**), where military spouses can share the books that speak to them and share their personal experiences.

Thanks also to the contributors at *The Military Spouse Book Review*: Terri Barnes (*Spouse Calls: Messages from a Military Life*); Jerri Bell (*It's My Country Too*); Amy Bermudez (*The Substance of Life*); Alison Buckholtz (*Standing By*); Emmy Curtis (*Aces Wild*); Mary Doyle (*Hidden Designs*); Simone Gorrindo (senior editor at *Vela Magazine*); Lauren Kay Halloran (*The Road Ahead*); Tiffany Hawk (*Love Me Anyway*); Caroline LeBlanc; Abby E. Murray (*How to Be Married After Iraq*); Leslie Hsu Oh (*Older Adults, Health Information, and the World Wide Web*); Kathleen M. Rodgers (*Seven Wings to Glory*); and Pastaveia St. John.

Thanks to Andria Williams (*The Longest Night*) and Angela Rickets (*No Man's War: Irreverent Confessions of an Infantry Wife*) for being awesome AWP roommates and friends.

Thanks to Ron Capps (*Seriously Not All Right: Five Wars in Ten Years*) for heading the Veterans Writing Project (**veteranswriting.org**) and to Peter Molin for giving me the wonderful opportunity to mentor other military writers.

Thanks to Peter Molin for hosting the Time Now blog (**acolytesofwar.com**) and for being the first to discuss my poetry in an academic essay.

Thanks to Jessica Melville Goodin for founding and hosting the Military Spouse Fine Artists Network (**milspofan.com**), where military spouses can network and find camaraderie.

Thanks to John Cathcart (*Delta 7*) and Maria Edwards (publisher at Navigator Books) for hosting the Facebook group "Military Writers, Poets, Visual & Performing Artists," where ideas and successes are shared.

Thanks to Eric Chandler (*Hugging This Rock: Poems of Earth & Sky, Love & War*) for sharing his high-flying, nature, parenting, and poetry adventures.

Thanks to Layla Lenhardt and the rest of the *1932 Quarterly* team for entrusting me as one of their assistant poetry editors.

Thanks to Eric Chandler; Siobhan Fallon; Dwight A. Gray; Pamela Hart; Lynn Marie Houston; Abby E. Murray; William Schuth; and Andria Williams for the kind words and support in their blurbs.

Thanks to Shel Silverstein; P.D. Eastman; Arnold Lobel; The Brothers Grimm; A. A. Milne; Munro Leaf; Heinrich Hoffman; Dr. Seuss; Oscar Wilde; Hans Christian Andersen; Patricia Scarry; Michael Bond; and Beatrix Potter for writing beautiful tales for children.

Thanks to Sun Tzu for writing such a poetic war manual.

Thanks to all those who read poetry.

Thanks to all those who read to children.

—Lisa Stice
Spring 2018

ABOUT THE WRITER

Lisa Stice is author of the previously published poetry collection *Uniform* (Aldrich Press, 2016), and a Pushcart Prize nominee. Her work is widely published in literary print and on-line journals. She volunteers as a mentor with the Washington, D.C.-based non-profit Veterans Writing Project; as an associate poetry editor with *1932 Quarterly*; and as a contributor for *The Military Spouse Book Review* (**www.militaryspousebookreview.com**).

The poet holds a Bachelor of Arts in English literature from Mesa State College (now Colorado Mesa University), Grand Junction, Colo., and a Master of Fine Arts in Creative Writing and Literary Arts from the University of Alaska, Anchorage.

Stice's work appears in anthologies including *Beyond the Hill* (Lost Tower Publications, 2017); and *Nuclear Impact: Broken Atoms in Our Hands* (Shabda Press, 2017).

In 2017, her poem "Dear Wadih Sa'adeh" was selected as an honorable mention in the poetry category in that year's volume of the *Proud to Be: Writing by American Warriors* anthology series, published by Southeast Missouri State University Press. Her poem "A Quick Lunch from the Noodle Stand" was nominated for the 2016 Pushcart Prize by *The Magnolia Review*.

While it is always difficult to say where home is, Stice says, the former high school teacher currently lives in North Carolina with her husband, daughter, and dog Seamus, a Norwich Terrier.

You can learn more about her on-line at:
lisastice.wordpress.com
facebook.com/LisaSticePoet

ABOUT THE COVER

Upper image, front cover:

The oil-on-canvas "Little Girl in Blue Armchair" was painted in 1878 by American artist Mary Stevenson Cassatt (1844–1926). Born in Pennsylvania, she spent most of her adult life in France. In Paris, 1877, she met Edgar Degas—one of the founders of the Impressionist movement—with whom she had a lifelong friendship and periods of professional collaboration in painting and print-making. She is celebrated for her tender yet unsentimental depictions of women in both public and private life, including moments of intimacy between mothers and children. Degas assisted in the painting of "Little Girl in Blue Armchair," and even supplied the human and canine models for the work. The girl was the daughter of a friend of Degas. The dog was a Brussels Griffon, a breed that remained a favorite of Cassatt's. In 1983, the painting was donated to the U.S. National Gallery of Art by Mr. and Mrs. Paul Mellon.

Lower image, front cover:

Nov. 29, 2017—U.S. Marine Cpl. David Ricketts, a combat engineer with Combat Logistics Detachment 5, Special Purpose Marine Air-Ground Task Force, Crisis Response, Central Command conduct a mounted convoy exercise utilizing the M240B and .50-cal. machine guns atop a Humvee while deployed in the Middle East. *U.S. Marine Corps photo by Sgt. Conner Robbins, Task Force 51/5th Marine Expeditionary Brigade*

Disclaimer: "The appearance of U.S. Department of Defense (DOD) visual information does not imply or constitute DOD endorsement."

Author photo (back cover) by Andria Williams, *Military Spouse Book Review*

DID YOU ENJOY THIS BOOK?

Tell your friends and family about it, or post your thoughts via social media sites, like Facebook and Twitter! On-line communities that serve military families, veterans, and service members are also ideal places to help spread the word about this book, and others like it!

You can also share a quick review on websites for other readers, such as Goodreads.com. Or offer a few of your impressions on bookseller websites, such as Amazon.com and BarnesandNoble.com!

Better yet, recommend the title to your favorite local librarian, poetry society or book club leader, museum gift store manager, or independent bookseller! There is nothing more powerful in business of publishing than a shared review or recommendation from a friend.

We appreciate your support! We'll continue to look for new stories and voices to share with our readers. Keep in touch!

You can write us at:

Middle West Press LLC
P.O. Box 31099
Johnston, Iowa 50131-9428

Or visit: **www.middlewestpress.com**

Other poetry collections from Middle West Press LLC:

Welcome to FOB Haiku:
War Poetry from Inside the Wire,
by Randy Brown, a.k.a. "Charlie Sherpa"

Hugging This Rock:
Poems of Earth & Sky, Love & War
by Eric Chandler